Fatal Mistakes in Home Buying & Real Estate Investment

If you don't make any of these mistakes, your success is guaranteed!

Bryan Law

Publisher: Fox College of Business

Although the author has researched all sources to ensure the accuracy and completeness of the information contained in this book, we assume no responsibility for error, inaccuracy, omission, or any inconsistency stated herein. Readers should consult a legal counsel and/or a professional in the related fields for specific applications to their individual situations.

First Edition – 2016

ISBN 978-0988121744

Preface

With more than twenty-five years of experience in real estate investment and teaching real estate courses, I have seen many successful cases of investing in real estate. On the other hand, I have also seen many failures which were due to uninformed decisions. Those people either bought the wrong type of property or simply missed the opportunity to make big profits from it.

Many of the mistakes made by those people stem from the myths shared among friends and relatives; as such, they can be avoided. The purpose of this book is to tell you the facts so that you can prevent those unfortunate failures from happening.

Enjoy reading, and good luck in investing!

Table of Contents

Introduction

Almost every commodity will grow in price over the years, so we have inflations. The prices of coffee, bread, and most goods have increased in the last few decades. Real estate prices have also increased multiple times since the last recession. However, not everyone who bought real estate in the last few decades has earned a profit by buying and selling. That is because they have made fatal mistakes in their home-buying and real estate investments.

The purchase of your home and any real estate investment is one of the most important decisions and also one of the most valuable investments that you have to make in your life. As a purchaser, especially a first-time homebuyer, there may be many questions in your mind. Common questions include:

Should I buy a house? Should I invest in real estate? If it is for my own use, should I buy or rent the property?

When is the best time to buy a house? Should I wait, or should I rush to buy it? What if the market crashes?

What if I cannot find a tenant and there is a vacancy? How long will the vacancy period last? How should I select a tenant?

What if the tenant does not pay rent? How do I evict the tenant? Will the process be a long battle?

Is the rate of return on real estate investment reasonable? How high a rate of return is reasonable? How should I calculate the true rate of return on real estate investment?

Is there any tax sheltering scheme that I may enjoy? How does it compare with other tax saving or tax deferring investment tools?

As each question is explored in depth, you will know how to avoid fatal mistakes in home buying and real estate investment.

1. Rent v. Own

Unlike stocks and mutual funds, real estate will never 'vanish'. Since it is real, you can have your personal control over it, but stocks and mutual funds consist of mere papers, and you may not have any right to make any decision in those corporations. On the other hand, unlike all other consumer goods that can be produced as much as you like in the factory, land has a limited supply and cannot be produced. Furthermore, land lasts forever and will never collapse. For these reasons, the value of a property will go up over the years.

Shelter is a basic necessity, so you are either renting or owning your home. As a result, the most common question is: Should I keep on renting or have my own house? Some people say the answer is obvious. They argue that the cost of paying rent is evidently greater than the cost of owning a house or condo unit because landlords can maintain a profit even after the deduction of mortgage and other related expenses. This answer is merely one of many, and no decision can be made based solely on this reasoning. In fact, each method of acquiring a home has advantages and disadvantages, and the requirements differ too. In general, we can summarize the basic pros and cons as follows:

Advantages of renting:

1. Less capital involved. Generally, all you have to pay up-front is the deposit of two months' rent or even less.

2. There may be a tax deduction for rent payments.

3. Flexible for relocation. Should you wish to move to another place, you can terminate the lease at the end of the term instead of selling your home.

4. Your borrowing power will not be lowered since no loan is involved in renting a house.

5. Better terms can typically be negotiated for a rental agreement than a loan (mortgage) agreement.

Disadvantages of renting:

1. Higher operating costs. Since the landlord has to make a profit on the lease, the costs of renting are higher than the costs of owning.

2. Loss of the opportunity to profit from appreciation at the end of the lease. Since a tenant does not own the property, they cannot enjoy the capital gain even if there is an increase in the value of the property.

3. Tenant has no right or limited right to make changes, even to something as simple as the wall colour.

Advantages of Owning:

1. Greater control of the property. You can do whatever you want, within the limits of the law, on the property you own.

2. Owners can enjoy potential capital growth.

3. There may be tax exemptions on capital gains and other possible tax benefits.

4. When there is a growth in the value of the property or an increase in your salary, you may be able to obtain more equity through refinancing.

5. Flexibility in ownership (joint tenants, tenants in common, etc).

Disadvantages of Owning:

1. The initial capital investment required (down payment, legal fee, etc) is much higher than two monthly rents.

2. The amount of money you can borrow and the ability to arrange financing vary, which can be a problem.

3. When you have a mortgage, your debt ratio goes up, which means that your borrowing power is weakened.

4. Selling costs can be high due to commissions and legal fees.

These are only the basic criteria for a decision. There are, of course, more factors to be considered before you can draw the final conclusion.

If you purchase your own property, you may enjoy other benefits. Borrowing money to purchase (leverage) and investing in your own mortgage are the two of them. We will discuss them one by one.

Borrowing money to invest in real estate is also known as leverage. Banks will not lend you money to invest in stocks or mutual funds, but they will do so to allow you to buy real estate, at least for your own house. Sometimes, the banks will lend you as much as 100% of the value of your house.

When you have around $1,500 in your pocket and want to invest it, it seems that you do not have many choices. Moreover, most investment tools have risks. Investing in your own mortgage is the best choice as it is 100% safe and rewarding. For example, you have a mortgage at an interest rate of 6.45% per year, with 25 years remaining. Your monthly payment will be $1,000.00, as shown in Schedule A.

Payment Schedule A
($1,000.00 P & I per month)

Month	Interest	Principal	Balance
11	$795.47	$204.53	$149,765.47
12	$794.38	$205.62	$149,559.85
13	$793.29	$206.71	$149,353.14
14	$792.19	$207.81	$149,145.33
15	$791.09	$208.91	$148,936.42
16	$789.98	$210.02	$148,726.40
17	$788.87	$211.13	$148,515.27
18	$787.75	$212.25	$148,303.02
19	$786.62	$213.38	$148,089.64
20	$785.49	$214.51	$147,875.13
21	$784.35	$215.65	$147,659.48
22	$783.21	$216.79	$147,442.69
23	$782.06	$217.94	$147,224.75
24	$780.90	$219.10	$147,005.65
25	$779.74	$220.26	$146,785.39
26	$778.57	$221.43	$146,563.96
27	$777.40	$222.60	$146,341.36
28	$776.22	$223.78	$146,117.58
29	$775.03	$224.97	$145,892.61
30	$773.84	$226.16	$145,666.45

Suppose you pay the mortgage of $1,541.90 more (the prepayment) in the twenty-first month. In that case, the original payment schedule will change to Payment Schedule B. You can see that when you make this prepayment of $1,541.90 in the twenty-first month, the remaining balance ($146,117.58) is equivalent to that in the twenty-eighth month in Payment Schedule A. That is, the payment schedule is shortened by seven months, resulting in more than $5,400 savings.

When you pay the twenty-second payment in Payment Schedule B, you actually pay the twenty-ninth payment in Payment Schedule A. In other words, you have saved seven monthly payments. You have instantly earned a return on investment of more than 350%!

Payment Schedule B

(Paid $1,541.90 more in the 21st month)

Month	Interest	Principal	Balance
11	$795.47	$204.53	$149,765.47
12	$794.38	$205.62	$149,559.85
13	$793.29	$206.71	$149,353.14
14	$792.19	$207.81	$149,145.33
15	$791.09	$208.91	$148,936.42
16	$789.98	$210.02	$148,726.40
17	$788.87	$211.13	$148,515.27
18	$787.75	$212.25	$148,303.02
19	$786.62	$213.38	$148,089.64
20	$785.49	$214.51	$147,875.13
21	$784.35	$215.65	$146,117.58
22	$775.03	$224.97	$145,892.61
23	$773.84	$226.16	$145,666.45
24	$772.64	$227.36	$145,439.09
25	$771.43	$228.57	$145,210.52
26	$770.22	$229.78	$144,980.74
27	$769.00	$231.00	$144,749.74
28	$767.78	$232.22	$144,517.52
29	$766.54	$233.46	$144,284.06
30	$765.31	$234.69	$144,049.37

Why is there a greater than 350% return on the $1,541.90 invested in (paid down) the mortgage? Simply put, it is because the $1,541.90 was repaid in the twenty-first month to lower the debt. In other words, the mortgage balance is reduced by $1,541.90 for the remaining amortization period. It will accumulate an astonishing interest by compounding the $1,541.90 at 6.45% annually for nearly 25 years. That is, the return is actually the savings in total interest payable for the $1,541.90 compounded over twenty-nine years.

When the mortgage interest rate is higher than 6.45% (say 15%), making a prepayment to your mortgage may result in a return of more than 30 times. That is, making a $1,000 prepayment may save you more than $30,000 in interest payment, which is over a 3,000% rate of return!

There are many more reasons why buying a property is more attractive than renting, and we will discuss them in the following chapters.

A rule of thumb is to always buy the property that you will live in or for your commercial use provided that you can afford it and will stay there for at least a few years.

Fatal Mistake #1

– Failing to buy the property you use for residential or commercial purposes.

2. The Real Estate Cycle

"Is it the right time to buy?" "Will the price drop soon?"

These are the most frequently asked questions in the real estate industry, especially when the market is hot, and people do not want to buy properties at the peak price. In order to answer the questions, we must understand the real estate cycle.

Whenever interest rates are low, and there is steady economic growth, the real estate markets will boom for a few years. This occurrence happens from time to time. Unfortunately, such a phenomenon gives false hope to some people that the real estate market will go up forever. As a result, many people buy houses to speculate without understanding the fundamentals of the real estate market. Most real estate speculators believed the market would continue rising when they bought real properties to flip. They did not know, or did not want to believe, that the real estate market follows a cycle.

It is important to understand that the real estate market follows a cycle. There are four phases in the cycle, namely: Recession, Recovery, Expansion and Oversupply.

Recession

This phase usually coincides with the economic recession. Prices of properties are at their lowest, and it is a buyer's market. Buying real estate at this time almost guarantees a profit when the market improves. Doing so is the axiom of 'buy low, sell high'. It is also the best time for first-time homebuyers to buy their homes since the price will be the most affordable one.

Recovery

The real estate market begins to recover; prices increase from the bottom of the curve.

Developers start to build as the prices may return to a profitable level to justify new construction. It is still the best time to buy, as prices are going up.

Expansion

It is still a good time to buy, as the rental market will be improving as well. Everyone in the market is buying, flipping and leasing. The best time to sell real estate is at the end of the expansion phase, as prices have reached the highest level.

Oversupply

In this phase, house prices and rents fall as there is an oversupply in the market. Real estate practitioners start developing niche markets and making acquisitions during the recession phase. Properties bought at this phase will need longer to reach the original price level once the market falls.

Timing the Cycle

If we can time the cycle to buy low and sell high effectively, we are guaranteed to make a profit. The real estate market becomes like a money printing machine! Unfortunately, the reality is that we will never be able to time the market.

Keeping in mind that a real estate cycle in North America may last for fifteen years or longer, we should expect it to take seven to ten years to recover if we buy real property at the peak of the cycle. Even if you buy a house at the peak time and you pay a high price for it, it really does not matter if you do not sell it until the next peak arrives. As a home, you will continue to live in the house with the same conditions regardless of whether its price goes up or down. As an investment, the property is profitable as long as it continues to generate a positive cash flow. As such, the crucial point is not when to buy a property; it is how long you can hold the property without selling it.

A newly wedded couple may plan to buy a bigger house within five years once they have children. At that time, if house prices go down, they will enjoy a lower price for the bigger house, although the one in which they are residing will be sold at a lower value, too. They still get the benefit as the money they save in buying a bigger house is more than the money they lose in selling a smaller house. If house prices go up, their existing house will likewise increase in value, making it easier for them to buy a larger house than those with no property on hand. This confirms what the first chapter says – you should always buy the property that you want to live in.

However, if you are not going to sell and buy another property (that is, you just want to sell the property for cash), or if you are downsizing, then you may have a loss if you do not hold the property for a period of long enough time.

A rule of thumb is to ensure you can hold the property as long as you want without having any financial difficulty so that you don't have to sell it unless you want to.

Fatal Mistake #2

– Failing to hold your property for a period of long enough time.

3. Vacancy

If the property you bought is for investment purposes, you will need a tenant to move in and pay you the rent.

It is the norm for commercial properties to have a lease term of three to ten years. For residential properties, you should ask for at least a one-year term. In both cases, a lease should be signed.

However, the vacancy rate in commercial units is higher than in residential units as not everybody manages a business, and not every business succeeds. This is particularly true during a recession.

You should know the differences between residential and commercial investment properties before buying. They are summarized as follows:

	Residential Properties	Commercial Properties
Examples	Condo units Townhouses Multiple complexes	Industrial units Strip plaza Store/Apartment
Typical Rate of Return	4% to 8%	6% to 12%
Typical Capital Investment	$25,000 and up	$250,000 and up
Typical Term of Lease	1 – 2 years	3 – 10 years
Type of rent	Most are gross rent (rent includes all expenses and tax)	Most are net rent (all expenses and taxes are extra)
Appraised Value	Determined by the neighbourhood of the property	Determined by the income generated by the property

Some people like to invest in a store plus an apartment in a well-developed area like a downtown core. This type of property averages out the advantages and disadvantages between residential and commercial properties. The potential for re-development is also a factor to consider.

If you are the user type buyer, that is, you are buying the house or commercial property for your own use, then you will have no problem with the vacancy issue. Your property will be 100% occupied by yourself. This is why you should always buy the property that you are using or in which you are residing to avoid fatal mistake #1.

All experienced developers know the importance of occupancy and that it may be difficult for commercial properties to be rented out. This is why they will not start constructing their commercial buildings without first having secured enough tenants; normally, they will only start construction after 70% of their units have been rented.

A rule of thumb is to never buy any commercial real estate for investment purposes that is not tenanted or if tenants are leaving soon. You will never know how long it will take to rent out the unit, which is a fatal mistake.

Fatal Mistake #3

– Failing to realize how crucial occupancy rates are in real estate investments.

4. Bad Debts

Once your property is rented out, you should have rental income from your tenant. However, the reality is not perfect, and the fact is you may have bad debt.

When your tenants have financial difficulties, they may pay you late or even may not pay at all. The consequence is that you will have a shortfall in rental income, even a negative cash flow. This may eventually affect your ability to pay the mortgage.

For commercial properties, it normally does not take long to evict the tenant for non-payment of rent. The effect of bad debts is minimal and leads only to vacancy. However, the problem will be more serious in residential properties.

In most jurisdictions, residential tenants are protected, and the landlords cannot evict the tenant for non-payment of rent without going through a lengthy process. Such processes can easily last for at least two to over six months if you are unfamiliar with the tenant eviction procedures. You will be lucky if the tenant moves out soon after their default in payment, as you do not have to deal with the tenant eviction process.

Again, you will not have a bad debt problem if you use the property yourself.

Many people think that leasing a commercial property to a stranger is not a big deal. They do not care about the credit history of the tenant, since the Landlord and Tenant Act does not apply to commercial or industrial properties. They can easily evict a tenant who is in default of payment. Let us review the following case.

Case Study

(Dollar amounts have been adjusted to reflect the value in today's market)

Betty is an experienced landlord who owns several commercial and industrial plazas. One day, a small unit of one of her industrial plazas became vacant, and she put a sign on the front door of the unit to lease it out. A young man approached her to rent it for a studio, and he was willing to pay the full price for which Betty had asked, with three months' rent as a deposit and one month's rent paid in advance. Betty felt the young man was decent, and the deposit was good enough to show that he was a reliable tenant. Betty leased the unit to the young man without any hesitation.

A few months later, the secretary told Betty that the young man was in default. Betty went to the unit and found that nothing was there except some garbage. She then dumped all the garbage in a bag and stored it for the young man to pick up. When Betty walked out of the unit, one of her tenants told her that the young man had only used the unit to sleep overnight and that no business had been opened since he had moved in. Although Betty sensed there might be something wrong, there was nothing she could do.

Betty then re-leased the unit to another company. One year later, the young man came to Betty's office saying that he had left a roll of film in the unit, which was priceless and asked for it. Betty told him nothing was there and just showed him a bag of garbage. He then sued Betty for the loss of the film and requested $750,000 as compensation for the damage.

Although Betty's lawyer found out that the young man was a habitual criminal, had just been released from jail before he made the claim, and that there were many contradictions in his testimony, Betty offered the young man a settlement. That was because the young man received legal aid while Betty had to pay her own legal fees, and her first legal bill had already exceeded $900,000 before going to court.

The case was settled by both parties; Betty spent over $950,000 in this litigation and paid $150,000 to the young man to settle so that he would drop the case.

The most important thing that Betty forgot to do was check the credit record of the young man, or at least ask for some references. Since the young man claimed that he was a photographer, there should have been some proof of his occupation (such as a work reference and reference letters from his clients). This omission cost Betty a lot.

A rule of thumb is to always pre-qualify your potential tenant; a check of credit, reference letter, and employment letter are must-haves, not nice-to-haves.

Fatal Mistake #4

– Failing to qualify your tenant, including failing to check their credit history.

5. *The Cash Flow*

Most stocks and mutual funds will not pay you dividends, but real estate will. Of course, it is not an actual dividend; rather, it is a cash flow generated from the tenancy. In fact, one of the advantages of real estate investment is that real estate can generate cash income (the rent), similar to the term deposit we have in a bank.

Since real estate generates monthly cash income, some people use it to replace annuities for their retirement plans. Unlike an annuity with a fixed amount of money and a limited number of payments, the cash you receive from rent will increase over the years and is a non-stop cash flow as long as you do not sell the property. Since the rent will be higher and higher, it means your cash flow will also be better and better.

Many investors have only one equation on their mind when deciding to buy real estate as an investment. They think the property will be a good income-generating property as long as its projected annual rent is high enough to pay the total annual mortgage payments, realty taxes and maintenance fees. They believe that since the rent collectible is high enough to pay all the above expenses, their investment is guaranteed and will make a reasonable profit over the years.

Using this strategy to invest in real estate is like gambling. There are usually some expenses that those investors have omitted to consider, such as agent's commission, maintenance cost, vacancy cost and bad debt. All of these 'forgotten' expenses may result in a negative income statement. When the real estate market is hot, they can sell the property and still make a profit. However, if the market is down, they will have to hold the property and lose money every year or sell it at a loss.

In order to analyze a real estate investment, we have to understand how the rate of return is calculated and study the cash flow.

There are many ways to calculate the rate of return on investment. The two most common and easiest methods in real estate are the capitalization rate and the cash on cash.

Simply speaking, the capitalization rate (cap rate) is the ratio between the annual net operating income and sale price. Net operating income is the total rent collected minus all expenses and allowances. A worksheet to help you calculate the net operating income and the cash flow is shown in Appendix A.

The higher the capitalization rate, the shorter the time needed to recover the capital (the purchase price). Usually, investors will look for properties with a cap rate of 8 percent or higher in a stable market, depending on the location of the properties. During the recession, people are buying at over 12%. In today's market, people are buying at around 5% only.

The formula for calculating the cap rate is given as:

$$\text{Capitalization rate} = \frac{\text{Annual net operating income}}{\text{Sale price of the property}}$$

The most common problem encountered in real estate investments is that the property cannot generate positive cash flow for its owner. The proper investment strategy is to ensure a positive rate of return from the property (which should be higher than the interest rate of a term deposit) so that the investor does not need to sell the properties under pressure. The investor should consider selling the properties only when the real estate market goes up, or the depreciation has been used up for sheltering taxes, but should never be under pressure to sell.

Before deciding whether or not to purchase an investment property, you must know not only how to calculate its cash flow but also how to project it for a couple of years. By projecting cash flow for a few years, you will know if you need extra money to 'feed' your property when it is 'hungry'. This projection is often called a cash flow analysis. A sample worksheet to assist you in doing a cash flow analysis on a property is shown in Appendix B.

Another question you should ask before buying a property is: Given that I have paid this amount of money (cash), how much cash income can this property produce for me? In order to compare the cash output from different properties, the rate "cash on cash" is applied instead of the cap rate. Actually, cash on cash is one of the yields of an investment. It is the ratio of the cash flow generated by the property to the money you have initially invested in that property. That is:

$$\text{Cash on cash} = \frac{\text{Cash flow before taxes}}{\text{Initial money invested}}$$

You can use the worksheet in Appendix A to calculate the cash flow before taxes. Once you know the cash flow before taxes generated by the property, you can find the cash-on-cash of it.

One day, an excited client showed me an advertisement in a local newspaper. It depicted a plaza for sale; she believed it would be a good investment. It was a three-unit, free-standing commercial plaza on a corner. The owner claimed the rate of return was 12 percent and asked for $1.1 million. It was located in the downtown core and had ample parking spaces.

It was too good to be true, as the market was looking for only an 8 percent rate of return at that time, so I called the owner to ask for details. After a detailed analysis, I found that the actual rate of return of that plaza was less than 7 percent, as the method the seller used was incorrect (maybe he intentionally did it wrong). Moreover, all leases were calculated in gross rent and on a monthly basis, which was not good for commercial properties. I therefore advised my client not to buy it.

The plaza was sold after one month, and I indirectly knew the new owner, who was a friend of my cousin's. My cousin told me soon after the closing date that one of the three tenants had moved out, and another tenant closed his business at the same time. This made the rate of return drop to less than 3 percent. Just when the new owner rented out the two units, he received a notice from the city saying that there would be a special assessment on his property, and the levy was $6,000. Since all the leases he signed were gross rent leases, that meant he had to pay the $6,000 himself.

Most commercial leases are based on net rent; therefore, realty taxes and maintenance fees are extra fees to be paid by the tenants. If the leases signed by the owner of the abovementioned plaza were all net-rented, he could have transferred the responsibility of paying the levy to his tenants so that he would not have to pay that $6,000.

A rule of thumb is to buy only properties with positive cash flow; do not buy any property that generates negative cash flow, which happens in many residential properties. For commercial properties, only buy those with net rent lease terms.

Fatal Mistake #5

– Failing to understand the importance of positive cash flow.

6. Tax Benefits

Under current tax rules in the United States, you can take an income tax deduction for all property taxes that you pay and for mortgage interest on both a first and a second home (with limits of one million one hundred thousand dollars worth of borrowing). That is, buying real estate may lower your total taxable income, especially with a mortgage on it. However, these tax rules do not apply in Canada.

Additionally, if the property is used as your principal residence, then its appreciation (capital gain by the increase in price) will be tax-free for the first $250,000 gain ($500,000 if you file joint returns). Based on this capital gain exemption, real estate will be, therefore, a very good 'retirement fund' if you have a large house for your family and sell the house to move to a smaller house when you retire. Some states, such as Florida, will provide extra tax benefits for real estate buyers or owners. In Canada, the profit you make by selling your primary residence will be 100% tax-free.

First-time homebuyers may be eligible for a mortgage interest credit if their income is below the median income for the area where they live. The purpose of such credit is to help lower-income individuals buy their own homes. A tax credit is allowed each year for part of the home mortgage interest you pay. In Canada, different provinces may have different programs to assist first-time homebuyers.

To apply for such credit in the United States, you must get a mortgage credit certificate (MCC) from your state or local government. Generally, an MCC is issued only in connection with a new mortgage for the purchase of your principal residence. You must contact the appropriate government agency about getting an MCC before you get a mortgage and before you buy your first home. However, since the laws are always changing, you should consult your accountant or lawyer for the most current tax laws in the state where you reside.

Some people will incorporate a company for the sole purpose of holding real estate. In addition to the benefits of limited liabilities to the owner, incorporation may result in further tax benefits when company shares are transferred to the buyer instead of selling the actual property. This is used in estate planning, too. Since different jurisdictions have different tax laws and real estate laws to govern such activity, you should consult your own legal counsel and accountant before taking such an approach. There may be more tax benefits on real estate trust funds that you may enjoy under the Taxpayer Relief Act. Again, you should consult a tax expert for the best tax-saving results.

Claiming depreciation (known as Modified Accelerated Cost Recovery System, MACRS, in the United States and known as Capital Cost Allowance, CCA, in Canada) is one of the tax benefits you may enjoy in real estate investment. By claiming the depreciation of your property, you may reduce your annual rental income so that you will end up paying less income tax. However, the depreciation that you claim may become a recapture when you sell the property, which will be treated as your income, resulting in a higher taxable income to you in the year that you sell the property.

<u>Example</u>

You have only one investment property, and the rental income is your only income source (you have no job). The annual net rent you receive is $30,000, and you may claim $6,000 depreciation each year. Although you can reduce your annual rental income by claiming depreciation, you should not do it if you plan to sell the property within a few years.

Say, if you have claimed $6,000 in depreciation each year for 5 years and you eventually sell the property at the end of the fifth year, you will have a recapture of $30,000. That means you will have $30,000 more income in that year. Since the tax rates in both Canada and the US are progressive, this means you will have to pay more tax money on the $30,000 recapture than the total of the five-year tax on the $6,000 you reduced each year.

A rule of thumb is to find out all the tax benefits and sheltering tools you may enjoy before buying real estate, but only apply those that are beneficial to you.

Fatal Mistake #6

– Failing to understand and utilize different kinds of tax saving and deferring tools.

Conclusion

Buying real estate is a long-term, safe and rewarding investment. It may be for your own use or to be rented out. Your first real estate investment should be your own house, as you will have all the following benefits:

- You will have the opportunity for capital growth over the years;

- You will pay a lower occupancy cost than renting;

- You will have no vacancy;

- You will have no bad debt;

- You will have no cash flow problem from the property;

- Your capital gain will be tax-exempt.

As long as you can afford it, you should buy the property that you are residing in (or a better property) instead of renting it, as you will lose many benefits if you are not the owner of the property.

Many people made mistakes not only in buying real estate but also made a mistake when they decided not to buy real estate. However, buying real estate as an investment should not be a rushed decision; you should do your homework in finding a good neighbourhood, shopping for a good financing tool, and targeting a good property.

If you do not own any property, buy one as your residence. Don't wait!

Appendix A

Annual Property Operating Data Form

Name _____ Date _____

Location _____ Price $ _____

Type of Property_____ Debt $ _____

Size of Property _____ Sq. Ft./Units   Equity $ _____

Mortgage	Amount	Payment	Interest	Term/Amt
1st	_____	_____	_____	_____
2nd	_____	_____	_____	_____
3rd	_____	_____	_____	_____

	$/Sq. Ft.	
ALL FIGURES ANNUAL	or $/Unit %	COMMENTS

Calculate the Income:

Potential Rental Income _____ _____

− Vacancy & Credit Losses _____ (___ % of above)

= Effective Rental Income _____ _____

+ Other Income _____ (parking, etc)

= Gross Operating Income _____ (Figure #1)

Calculate the Expenses:

Real Estate Taxes _____ _____

+ Property Insurance _____ _____

+ Off-Site Management _____ _____

+ Payroll On-site Personnel _____ _____

+ Expenses / Benefits _____ _____

+ Taxes _____ _____

+ Repair and Maintenance   _____   _____

+ Utilities

     Water   _____   _____

     Electricity   _____   _____

     Gas / Oil   _____   _____

     Others   _____   _____

+ Accounting   _____   _____

+ Legal   _____   _____

+ Leasing Commission   _____   _____

+ Advertising/Licenses/Permits   _____   _____

+ Supplies   _____   _____

+ Miscellaneous   _____   _____

                          _____   _____

                          _____   _____

= Total Operating Expenses   _____   (Figure #2)

Calculate the Cash Flow:

   Gross Operating Income (Figure #1)   _____

− Total Operating Expenses (Figure #2)   _____

+ Additional Rent Paid by Tenant (if any)   _____

= Net Operating Income   _____

− Annual Debt Service (Mortgage Payment)   _____

= Cash Flow Before Tax   _____

Appendix B

Cash Flow Analysis Form

Property Name: _____

Down Payment: _____ + Acquisition Costs: _____

= Investment at Purchase: _____ + Debt: _____

= Acquisition Price: _____

Mortgage Data

Mortgage Data	Beginning Balance	Term/ Amort'n	# payments per year	Interest Rate	Payment	A.D.S	Remarks
1st Mort							
2nd Mort							

Taxable Income

		Year 1	Year 2	Year 3	Year 4	Year 5
	Potential Rental Income					
Minus:	Vacancy & Credit Losses					
Equals:	Effective Rental Income					
Plus:	Other Income					
Equals:	Gross Operating Income					
Minus:	Operating Expenses					
Equals:	**Net Operating Income**					
Minus:	Non-Operating Expense					
Minus:	Interest – 1st Mortgage					
Minus:	Interest – 2nd Mortgage					
Minus:	Interest – 3rd Mortgage					
Minus:	Amortization of Loan Fees					
Equals:	Taxable Income Before CCA					
Minus:	Allowable CCA					
Equals:	Real Estate Taxable Income					
Times:	Marginal Tax Rate					
Equals:	**Tax Liability**					

Cash Flows

		Year 1	Year 2	Year 3	Year 4	Year 5
Net Operating Income						
Minus:	Annual Debt Service (1st)					
	Annual Debt Service (2nd)					
Equals:	Cash Flow Before Taxes					
Minus:	Tax Liability					
=	**Cash Flows After Tax**					

~ The End ~